Title page

Diamond rules to acquire&retain wealth

Attract Good Luck, Wealth and Abundance

Hi

My name is Deviana sharon S. the author, content editor, content strategist, from india, but live in the US, and i dedicate this website to the ascended masters, saint germain, lady portia, angels, devas, fairies &animal totems that have helped me in my journey to ascension in this lifetime balancig 51%negative karma in 25 years and fulfilling my full and highest divine plan and potential, Dharma(soul purpose), RIGHTFUL DUTY, and karma to make my ascension with my twin flame berkeley in this lifetime a retired US military veteran Seargeant and broadcasting journalism degree pursuerBA final year and a writer by trade, similar age to me. I am a Author, publisher, artcle/content editor, content strategist and Publish books and ebooks, bookseller, im also a business owner, founder&director of sharon&berkeley real estate investments LLP india, also owning the brand and shopify store of Sharon&berkeley Excellence doing th right thing advantage of the witch&the raven and this website/store, and have a BA in psychology from minot state university with philosophy minor&broadcasting concentration

please also visit my website sites.google.com/view/winningmindsetosuccess/home and also
https://sharon-berkeley-Excellence-do-the-right-thing-advantage.myshopify.com to buy my books, music under my brand and all niche specific products on self improvement-law of attraction,manifestation,magick,feng shui,mental health.2)health&wellness
3)fitness,natural remedies to weight gain&weight loss products.will be adding more niches soon.

A person's fortune is changed

through the mind a persons mind

is changed through the power of

repetition

By Deviana Sharon seelam

Lawful Notification

The Distributer has strived to be as precise and finish as conceivable in the making of this report, despite the way that he doesn't warrant or speak to whenever that the substance inside are exact because of the quickly changing nature of the Web.

The Distributer won't be answerable for any misfortunes or harms of any sort brought about by the peruser whether straightforwardly or in a roundabout way emerging from the utilization of the data found in this report.

This report isn't planned for use as a wellspring of lawful, business, bookkeeping or monetary counsel. All perusers are instructed to look for administrations regarding able experts in legitimate, business, bookkeeping, and money field.

Peruser accepts accountability for utilization of data contained in this. The creator claims all authority to make changes without notice. The Distributer accepts no accountability or risk at all for the benefit of the peruser of this manual.

The Brilliant Standards of Securing Riches

In the US where there is more land than individuals, it isn't at all hard for people healthy to bring in cash. In this relatively new field there are such countless roads of progress open, such countless jobs which are not packed, that any individual of either sex who is willing, at any rate for the present, to take part in any decent occupation that offers, may discover rewarding work.

The individuals who truly want to achieve autonomy, have just to set their psyches upon it, and receive the legitimate methods, as they do as to whatever other item which they wish to achieve, and the thing is handily done. Yet, anyway simple it very well might be found to bring in cash, I have no uncertainty a large number of my listeners will concur it is the most troublesome thing on the planet to keep it. The way to abundance is, as Dr. Franklin genuinely says, "as plain as the way to the plant." It comprises basically in exhausting short of what we acquire; that is by all accounts an exceptionally straightforward issue. Mr. Micawber, one of those upbeat manifestations of the amicable Dickens, places the case in a solid light when he says that to have yearly pay of twenty pounds for each annum, and burn through twenty pounds and sixpence, is to be the most hopeless of men; while, to have a pay of just twenty pounds, and spend yet nineteen pounds and sixpence is to be the most joyful of humans. A significant number of my perusers may state, "we get this: this is economy, and we realize economy is riches; we realize we can't eat our cake and keep it too." Yet maybe more instances of disappointment emerge from botches on this point than practically some other. The truth of the matter is, numerous individuals think they comprehend economy when they truly don't.

Genuine economy is misunderstood, and individuals experience existence without appropriately fathoming what that guideline is. One says, "I have a pay of such a huge amount of, and here is my neighbor who has the equivalent; yet consistently he stretches something beyond and I miss the mark; for what reason right? I thoroughly understand economy." He figures he does, yet he doesn't. There are men who believe that economy comprises in saving cheddar parings and light finishes, in cutting off two pence from the laundress' bill and doing a wide range of close to nothing, mean, grimy things. Economy isn't ugliness. The setback is, additionally, that this class of people let their economy apply just a single way. They extravagant they are so superbly efficient in saving a half-penny where they should burn through two pence, that they want to stand to waste in different ways.

Before lamp oil was found or considered, one may stop for the time being at practically any rancher's home in the rural locale and get an excellent dinner, however after dinner he may endeavor to peruse in the parlor, and would think that its incomprehensible with the wasteful light of one flame. The lady, seeing his difficulty, would state: "It is fairly hard to peruse here nights; the axiom says 'you should have a boat adrift to have the option to consume two candles immediately; we never have an additional flame besides on additional events." These additional events happen, maybe, double a year. In this manner the great lady saves five, six, or ten dollars in that time: however the data which may be gotten from having the additional light would, obviously, far exceed a huge load of candles.

However, the difficulty doesn't end here. Feeling that she is so practical in fat confections, she wants to stand to go oftentimes to the town and burn through twenty or thirty dollars for strips and furbelows, a significant number of which are a bit much. This bogus indicate may every now and again be found in men of business, and in those occasions it frequently rushes to composing paper. You discover great finance managers who save all the old envelopes and scraps, and would not tear another piece of paper, on the off chance that they could stay away from it, for the world. This is all well indeed; they may in this way save five or ten dollars every year, except being so conservative (just in note paper), they want to bear to sit around; to host costly gatherings, and to drive their carriages. This is a delineation of Dr. Franklin's "saving at the nozzle and squandering at the bung-opening;" "not great with finances." Punch in discussing this "one thought" class of individuals says "they resemble the one who purchased a penny herring for his family's supper and afterward recruited a mentor and four to take it home." I never realized a man to prevail by rehearsing this sort of economy.

Genuine economy comprises in continually causing the pay to surpass the out-go. Wear the old garments somewhat more if essential; get rid of the new pair of gloves; retouch the old dress: live on plainer food if need be; so that, under all conditions, except if some unexpected mishap happens, there will be an edge for the pay. A penny here, and a dollar there, put at revenue, continues collecting, and in this way the ideal outcome is achieved. It requires some preparation, maybe, to achieve this economy, however when once accustomed to it, you will discover there is more fulfillment in levelheaded saving than in silly spending.

Here is a formula which I suggest: I have discovered it to work a phenomenal remedy for excess, and particularly for mixed up economy. At the point when you find that you have no excess toward the year's end, but have a decent pay, I encourage you to take a couple of pieces of paper and structure them into a book and discount each thing of use. Post it consistently or week in two sections, one headed "necessaries" or even "solaces", and the other headed "extravagances," and you will find that the last segment will be twofold, high pitch, and oftentimes multiple times more prominent than the previous. The genuine solaces of life cost yet a

little part of what a large portion of us can procure. It is the eyes of others and not our own eyes which ruin us. On the off chance that all the world were visually impaired aside from myself l ought not enjoy fine garments or furniture." In America numerous people like to rehash "we are largely free and equivalent," however it is an incredible misstep in a bigger number of faculties than one.

That we are conceived "free and equivalent" is a brilliant truth in one sense, yet we are not all brought into the world similarly rich, and we never will be.

One may state; "there is a man who has a pay of 50,000 dollars for each annum, while I have yet 1,000 dollars; I realized that individual when he was helpless such as myself; presently he is rich and thinks he is superior to I am; I will show him that I am in the same class as he; I will proceed to purchase a pony and cart; no, I can't do that, however I will proceed to employ one and ride this evening on the very street that he does, and accordingly demonstrate to him that I am on a par with he."

My companion, you need not take that inconvenience; you can undoubtedly demonstrate that you are "on a par with he;" you have just to act just as he does; yet you can't cause anyone to accept that you are rich as he may be. Also, in the event that you put on these "airs," add burn through your time and go through your cash, your helpless spouse will be obliged to clean her fingers off at home, and get her tea two ounces all at once, and all the other things in extent, all together that you may keep up "appearances," and, all things considered, bamboozle no one. Then again, Mrs. Smith may state that her nearby neighbor wedded Johnson for his cash, and "everyone says as much." She has a decent

1,000 dollar camel's hair wrap, and she will cause Smith to get her an impersonation one, and she will sit in a seat directly close to her neighbor in chapel, to demonstrate that she is her equivalent.

My great lady, you won't excel on the planet, if your vanity and jealousy accordingly start to lead the pack. In this nation, where we accept the greater part should govern, we disregard that guideline with respect to design, and let a modest bunch of individuals, considering themselves the nobility, run up a bogus norm of flawlessness, and in attempting to ascend to that norm, we continually keep ourselves poor; all the time burrowing ceaselessly for outside appearances. How much more astute to be a "law unto ourselves" and state, "we will manage our out-pass by our pay, and lay up something for a blustery day." Individuals should be as reasonable regarding the matter of cash getting as on some other subject. Like causes produces like impacts. You can't gather a fortune by taking the street that prompts neediness. It needs no prophet to disclose to us that the individuals who live completely up to their methods, with no thought about a converse in this life, can never achieve a financial freedom.

People familiar with satisfy each impulse and fancy, will think that its hard, from the outset, to chop down their different pointless costs, and will feel it an incredible abstemiousness to live in a more modest house than they have been acquainted with, with more affordable furnishings, less organization, less exorbitant garments, less workers,

less number of balls, parties, theater-goings, carriage-ridings, joy outings, stogie smokings, alcohol drinkings, and different luxuries; however, all things considered, on the off chance that they will attempt the arrangement of laying by a "savings," or, as such, a little amount of cash, at premium or prudently put resources into land, they will be astounded at the they will be amazed at the delight to be gotten from continually adding to their little "heap," just as from all the affordable propensities which are incited by this course.

The old suit of garments, and the old hood and dress, will respond in due order regarding another season; the Croton or spring water taste in a way that is better than champagne; a virus shower and a lively walk will demonstrate more elating than a ride in the best mentor; a social visit, a night's perusing in the family circle, or an hour's play of "chase the shoe" and "visually impaired man's buff" will be undeniably more wonderful than a fifty or 500 dollar party, when the reflection on the distinction in expense is enjoyed by the individuals who start to know the joys of saving. A great many men are kept poor, and several thousands are made so after they have procured very adequate to help them well through life, in outcome of laying their arrangements of living on too expansive a stage. A few families exhaust as much as 20,000 dollars for every annum, and some significantly more, and would hardly realize how to live on less, while others secure more strong happiness habitually on a 20th piece of that sum. Success is a more extreme experience than difficulty, particularly abrupt thriving. "What was easy to get is just as easy to lose," is an old and genuine saying. A feeling of pride and vanity, when allowed to have full influence, is the undying blister worm which chews the very vitals of a man's common belongings, let them be little or extraordinary, hundreds, or millions. Numerous people, as they succeed, quickly grow their thoughts and initiate exhausting for extravagances, until in a brief timeframe their costs gobble up their pay, and they become destroyed in their silly endeavors to keep up appearances, and make a "sensation."

A man of his word of fortune who says, that when he initially started to flourish, his significant other would have another and rich couch. "That couch," he says, "cost me 30,000 dollars!" When the couch arrived at the house, it was discovered important to get seats to coordinate; at that point side-sheets, covers and tables "to relate" with them, etc through the whole load of furniture; when finally it was discovered that the house itself was excessively little and antiquated for the furnishings, and another one was worked to compare with the new buys; "in this way," added my companion, "summarizing a cost of 30,000 dollars, brought about by that solitary couch, and outfitting on me, looking like workers, hardware, and the essential costs chaperon after keeping up a fine 'foundation,' a yearly expense of eleven thousand dollars, and a tight squeeze at that: though, ten years prior, we lived with substantially more genuine solace, on the grounds that with considerably less consideration, on the same number of hundreds. In all actuality," he proceeded, "that couch would have carried me to inescapable insolvency, had not a most unexampled title to flourishing kept me above it, and had I not checked the normal longing to 'cut a scramble'."

The establishment of accomplishment in life is acceptable wellbeing: that is the base fortune; it is likewise the premise of bliss. An individual can't aggregate a fortune very well when he is debilitated. He has no aspiration; no motivator; no power. Obviously, there are the individuals who have terrible wellbeing and can't resist: you can't expect that such people can gather riches, however there are a considerable number of in chronic weakness who need not be so.

Assuming, at that point, sound wellbeing is the establishment of progress and bliss throughout everyday life, how significant it is that we should examine the laws of wellbeing, which is nevertheless another articulation for the laws of nature! The closer we keep to the laws of nature, the closer we are to acceptable wellbeing, but the number of people there are who give no consideration to regular laws, yet totally violate them, even against their own normal tendency. We should realize that the "wrongdoing of obliviousness" is never winked at with respect to the infringement of nature's laws; their infraction consistently brings the punishment. A youngster may push its finger into the flares without realizing it will consume, thus endures, apology, even, won't stop the savvy. A significant number of our precursors knew almost no about the standard of ventilation. They didn't think a lot about oxygen, whatever other "gin" they may have been familiar with; and thus they constructed their homes with minimal seven-by-nine feet rooms, and these old fashioned devout Puritans would secure themselves up one of these cells, express their petitions and hit the sack. Toward the beginning of the day they would sincerely restore a debt of gratitude is in order for the "safeguarding of their lives," during the evening, and no one would be wise to motivation to be appreciative. Presumably some large break in the window, or in the entryway, let in a little natural air, and in this way saved them.

Numerous people purposely disregard the laws of nature against their better motivations, for design. For example, there is one thing that nothing living aside from a despicable worm actually normally cherished, and that is tobacco; yet the number of people there are who purposely train an unnatural craving, and defeat this embedded abhorrence for tobacco, so much that they will adore it. They have hold of a noxious, dirty weed, or rather that takes a firm hold of them. Here are hitched men who run about spitting tobacco juice on the rug and floors, and here and there even upon their spouses other than. They don't kick their spouses out of entryways like inebriated men, however their wives, I have no uncertainty, frequently wish they were outside of the house. Another unsafe element is that this counterfeit craving, similar to envy, "develops by what it benefits from;" when you love what is unnatural, a more grounded hunger is made for the pernicious thing than the common longing for what is innocuous. There is an old axiom which says that "propensity is natural," however a fake propensity is more grounded than nature. Take for example, an old tobacco-chewer; his affection for the "quid" is more grounded than his adoration for a specific sort of food. He can surrender cook hamburger simpler than surrender the weed.

Youthful fellows lament that they are not men; they might want to hit the hay young men and wake up men; and to achieve this they duplicate the negative behavior patterns of their seniors. Little Tommy and Johnny see their dads or uncles smoke a line, and they state, "In the event that I could just do that, I would take care of business as well; uncle John has gone out and left his line of tobacco, let us attempt it." They take a match and light it, and afterward puff away. "We will figure out how to smoke; do you like it Johnny?" That fellow dejectedly answers: "Not without question; it tastes severe;" before long he develops pale, yet he endures dry he before long proposals up a penance on the special raised area of style; however the young men stick to it and continue on until finally they overcome their common cravings and become the survivors of gained tastes.

Take the tobacco-chewer. Toward the beginning of the day, when he gets up, he places a quid in his mouth and keeps it there the entire day, never taking it out but to trade it for a new one, or when he will eat; goodness! truly, at stretches during the day and night, numerous a chewer takes out the quid and grasps it adequately long to take a beverage, and afterward pop it returns once more. This basically demonstrates that the craving for rum is significantly more grounded than that for tobacco. At the point when the tobacco-chewer goes to your nation seat and you show him your grapery and organic product house, and the wonders of your nursery, when you offer him some new, ready natural product, and state, "Old buddy, I have here the most scrumptious apples, and pears, and peaches, and apricots; I have imported them from Spain, France and Italy—simply observe those tasty grapes; there isn't anything more flavorful nor more solid than ready organic product, so help yourself; I need to see you please yourself with these things;" he will roll the dear quid under his tongue and answer, "No, I thank you, I have tobacco in my mouth."

His sense of taste has gotten narcotized by the harmful weed, and he has lost, in an incredible measure, the fragile and lucky preference for natural products. This shows what costly, pointless and harmful propensities men will get into. I talk for a fact. I have smoked until I shuddered like an aspen leaf, the blood raced to my head, and I had a palpitation of the heart which I thought was coronary illness, till I was nearly slaughtered with alarm. At the point when I counseled my doctor, he said "sever tobacco utilizing." I was not just harming my wellbeing and going through a lot of cash, however I was setting a terrible model. I complied with his advice. No youngster on the planet ever looked so wonderful, as he suspected he did, behind a fifteen penny stogie or a meerschaum!

These comments apply with ten times power to the utilization of inebriating drinks. To make cash, requires an unmistakable cerebrum. A man must see that two and two make four; he should lay every one of his arrangements with reflection and thinking ahead, and intently look at all the subtleties and the intricate details of business. As no man can prevail in business except if he has a cerebrum to empower him to lay his arrangements, and motivation to direct him in their execution, along these lines, regardless of how abundantly a man might be honored with

knowledge, if the mind is jumbled, and his judgment distorted by inebriating drinks, it is unimaginable for him to carry on business effectively. The number of good open doors have passed, never to return, while a man was tasting a "social glass," with his companion! The number of stupid deals have been made affected by the "nervine," which briefly makes its casualty think he is rich. The number of significant possibilities have been postponed until to-morrow, and afterward perpetually, on the grounds that the wine cup has tossed the framework into a condition of stupor, killing the energies so basic to accomplishment in business. Verily, "wine is a charlatan." The utilization of inebriating drinks as a refreshment, is as much a fascination, just like the smoking of opium by the Chinese, and the previous is very as dangerous to the achievement of the finance manager as the last mentioned.

DON'T MISJUDGE YOUR VOCATION

The most secure arrangement, and the one generally certain about progress for the youngster beginning throughout everyday life, is to choose the job which is generally amicable as he would prefer. Guardians and gatekeepers are frequently too careless with respect to this. It extremely normal for a dad to state, for instance: "I have five young men. I will make Billy a minister; John a legal counselor; Tom a specialist, and Dick a rancher." He at that point goes into town and looks going to perceive how he will do Sammy. He gets back and says "Sammy, I see watch-production is a pleasant refined business; I figure I will make you a goldsmith." He does this, paying little mind to Sam's common tendencies, or virtuoso.

We are all, no uncertainty, conceived for a shrewd reason. There is as much variety in our minds as in our faces. Some are brought into the world common mechanics, while some have extraordinary abhorrence for hardware. Let twelve young men of ten years get together, and you will before long notice a few are "shaving" out some bright gadget; working with locks or convoluted hardware. At the point when they were nevertheless five years of age, their dad could discover no toy to please them like a riddle. They are common mechanics; however the other eight or nine young men have various aptitudes. I have a place with the last class; I never had the smallest love for component; actually, I have such a hatred for confounded apparatus. I never had resourcefulness enough to shave a juice tap so it would not hole. I never could make a pen that I could compose with, or comprehend the guideline of a steam motor. On the off chance that a man was to accept such a kid as I seemed to be, and endeavor to make a watchmaker of him, the kid may, after an apprenticeship of five or seven years, have the option to dismantle and assemble a watch; however all through life he would be stirring up slope and

holding onto each reason for leaving his work and sitting ceaselessly his time. Watch making is shocking to him.

Except if a man enters upon the employment planned for him commonly, and most appropriate to his impossible to miss virtuoso, he will fail. I am happy to accept that most of people do locate their correct work. However we see numerous who have mixed up their calling, from the metalworker up (or down) to the priest. You will see, for example, that unprecedented etymologist the "educated smithy," who should have been an educator of dialects; and you may have seen attorneys, specialists and priests who were better fitted naturally for the iron block or the lap stone.

RIGHT PLACE, RIGHT TIME -SYNCHRONICITY

Subsequent to making sure about the correct area, you should be mindful so as to choose the legitimate area. You may have been equipped to deal with a lodging guardian, and they state it requires a virtuoso to "realize how to keep an inn." You may direct an inn predictably, and give sufficiently to 500 visitors consistently; yet, on the off chance that you ought to find your home in a little town where there is no railroad correspondence or public travel, the area would be your ruin.

It is similarly significant that you don't initiate business where there are as of now enough to fulfill all needs in a similar occupation.

AVOID DEBT LIKE A BUBONIC PLAGUE

Youngsters beginning in life ought to try not to run into obligation. That is guaranteed. There is hardly whatever else that hauls an individual down like obligation. It is a subjugated situation to get sick, yet we find numerous a youngster, scarcely out of his "adolescents," running paying off debtors (and truly, this has been continuing for quite a long time for as far back as men and history could recall). He meets a mate and says, "Take a gander at this: I have trusted for another suit of garments." He appears to view the garments as such a huge amount of given to him; all things considered, it regularly is thus, in any case, in the event that he prevails with regards to paying and, at that point gets trusted once more, he is receiving a propensity which will keep him in neediness through life. Obligation loots a man of his sense of pride, and makes him nearly scorn himself.

Snorting and moaning and working for what he has eaten up or exhausted, and now when he is called upon to settle up, he has nothing to show for his cash; this is appropriately named "working for a dead pony." I don't talk about vendors purchasing and selling using a loan, or of the individuals who purchase on layaway to turn the buy to a benefit.

Cash is in certain regards like fire; it is a fantastic worker however a horrible expert. At the point when you make them ace you; when interest is continually accumulating against you, it will hold you down in the most noticeably awful sort of subjugation. Be that as it may, let cash work for you, and you have the most committed worker on the planet. It is no "eye-worker." There is not much or lifeless that will work so dependably as cash when put at revenue, all around made sure about. It works night and day, and in wet or dry climate.

So don't allow it to neutralize you; on the off chance that you do there is zero chance for achievement in life most definitely.

PERSEVERENCE IS REALLY ANOTHER WORD FOR SELF-RELIANCE AND SELF DEPENDANCE

At the point when a man is in the correct way, he should continue on. I discuss this in light of the fact that there are a few people who are "brought into the world tired;" normally apathetic and having no confidence and no persistence. Be that as it may, they can develop these characteristics, as Davy Crockett stated:

"This thing recollect, when I am dead: Be certain you are correct, at that point proceed."

It is this thumbs up compulsion, this assurance not to let the detestations or the blues claim you, to cause you to loosen up your energies in the battle for freedom, which you should develop.

The number of have nearly arrived at the objective of their desire, in any case, losing confidence in themselves, have loosened up their energies, and the brilliant prize has been lost until the end of time.

It is, no uncertainty, frequently evident, as Shakespeare says:

"There is a tide in the issues of men, Which, taken at the flood, leads on to fortune."

On the off chance that you waver, some bolder hand will loosen up before you and get the prize. Recall the maxim of Solomon: "He becometh helpless that dealeth with a leeway hand; however the hand of the persistent maketh rich."

Determination is at times however another word for confidence. Numerous people normally look on the clouded side of life, and get inconvenience. They are conceived so. At that point they request exhortation, and they will be represented by one breeze and passed up another, and can't depend upon themselves. Until you can get with the goal that you can depend upon yourself, you need not anticipate succeeding.

Men who have met with monetary turns around, and totally ended it all, since they figured they would never beat their setback. Yet, I have known other people who have met more genuine monetary troubles, and have spanned them over by basic persistence, supported by a firm conviction that they were doing evenhandedly, and that Fortune would "conquer evil with great."

You will see this showed in any circle of life.

WHATEVER YOU DO, DO IT WITH ALL YOUR MIGHT

Work at it, if vital, early and late, in season and unavailable, not leaving a stone unturned, and never conceding for a solitary hour that which should be possible similarly too now. The old saying is brimming with truth and signifying, "Whatever merits doing by any stretch of the imagination, merits progressing admirably." Numerous a man gains a fortune by doing his business completely, while his neighbor stays poor forever, on the grounds that he just half does it. Desire, energy, industry, diligence, are crucial essentials for accomplishment in business.

Fortune consistently favors the fearless, and never helps a man who doesn't help himself. It won't do to invest your energy like Mr. Micawber, in trusting that something will "turn up." To such men one of two things for the most part "turns up:" the poorhouse or the prison; for inertness breeds unfortunate propensities, and garments a man in clothes. The helpless high-roller drifter says to a rich man:

"I have found there is sufficient cash on the planet for us all, in the event that it was similarly isolated; this should be done, and we will all be content."

"In any case, was the reaction, "if everyone resembled you, it would be gone through in two months, and what might you do at that point?"

"Goodness! Separation once more; continue isolating, obviously!"

I was as of late perusing in a London paper a record of a like rational beggar who was kicked out of a modest motel since he was unable to take care of his tab, however he had a move of papers standing out of his jacket pocket, which, upon assessment, end up being his arrangement for taking care of the public obligation of Britain without the guide of a penny.

Individuals must do as Cromwell stated: "trust in Provision, however keep the powder dry." Do your piece of the work, or you will fail. Mahomet, one evening, while at the same time settling in the desert, caught one of his exhausted supporters comment: "I will free my camel, and trust it to God!" "No, no, not really," said the prophet, "tie thy camel, and trust it to God!" Do everything you can for yourselves, and afterward trust to Fortune, or karma, or whatever you please to call it, for the rest.

DEPEND UPON YOUR OWN PERSONAL EXERTIONS AND TALENTS
The eye of the business is frequently worth more than the hands of twelve workers.

In the idea of things, a specialist can't be so devoted to his manager as to himself. Numerous who are businesses will bring to mind occurrences where the best representatives have ignored significant focuses which couldn't have gotten away from their own perception as an owner. No man has a privilege to hope to prevail in life except if he comprehends his business, and no one can comprehend his business completely except if he learns it by close to home application and experience. A man might be a producer: he must become familiar with the numerous subtleties of his business by and by; he will master something consistently, and he will discover he will commit errors virtually consistently. What's more, these very mix-ups are serves to him in the method of encounters in the event that he however regards them. He will resemble the Yankee tin-vendor, who, having been cheated as to quality in the acquisition of his product, stated: "Okay, there's a little data to be picked up each day; I will never be cheated in that way again." In this manner a man purchases his experience, and it is the best kind if not bought at too dear a rate.

Among the proverbs of the senior Rothschild was one, all clear Catch 22:

"Be wary and strong." This is by all accounts a logical inconsistency in wording, however it isn't, and there is incredible astuteness in the saying. It is, truth be told, a dense articulation of what I have just said. It is to state; "you should practice your alert in laying your arrangements, yet be strong in doing them." A man who is everything alert, will never set out to grab hold and be effective; and a man who is all intensity, is only careless, and should in the end fall flat. A man may go on '"change" and make fifty, or 100,000 dollars in guessing in stocks, at a solitary activity. Be that as it may, in the event that he has basic intensity without alert, it is simple possibility, and what he gains to-day he will lose to-morrow. You should have both the alert and the intensity, to guarantee achievement.

The Rothschilds have another proverb: "have nothing to do with an unfortunate man or spot." (This specific adage is additionally talked about in the 48 Laws of Intensity). In other words, have nothing to do with a man or spot which never succeeds, on the grounds that, in spite of the fact that a man may seem, by all accounts, to be straightforward and canny, yet in the event that he attempts either thing and consistently comes up short, it is because of some flaw or ailment that you will be unable to find yet by and by which should exist.

There is nothing of the sort on the planet as karma. There never was a man who could go out toward the beginning of the day and discover a tote brimming with gold in the road to-day, and another to-morrow, etc, for quite a while: He may do so once in his life; yet most definitely, he is as obligated to lose it as to discover it. "Like causes produce like impacts." If a man receives the appropriate techniques to be effective, "karma" won't forestall him. In the event that he doesn't succeed, there are purposes behind it, albeit, maybe, he will most likely be unable to see them.

USE THE BEST TOOLS

Men in drawing in representatives should be mindful so as to get the best. Comprehend, you can't have too great instruments to work with, and there is no apparatus you should be so specific probably as living devices. On the off chance that you get a decent one, it is smarter to keep him, than continue evolving. He masters something consistently; and you circular segment profited by the experience he gains. He is worth more to you this year than last, and he is the last man to leave behind, if his propensities are acceptable, and he proceeds with dependable. On the off chance that, as he gets more important, he requests an excessive increment of compensation; on the notion that you can't manage without him, let him go. When and if at any point you have such a worker, consistently release him; first, to persuade him that his place may

be provided, and second, since he is worthless on the off chance that he thinks he is priceless and can't be saved.

In any case, you would keep him, if conceivable, to benefit from the consequence of his experience. A significant component in a representative is the mind. You can see charges up, "Hands Needed," however "hands" are not worth an extraordinary arrangement without "heads."

Those men who have minds and experience are hence the most important and not to be promptly left behind; it is better for them, just as yourself, to keep them, at sensible advances in their pay rates occasionally.

DON'T GET ABOVE YOUR BUSINESS AND WHAT YOURE FOCUSED ON

Youngsters after they traverse their business preparing, or apprenticeship, rather than seeking after their side interest and ascending in their business, will frequently lie about sitting idle. They state; "I have taken in my business, yet I won't be a worker; what is the object of learning my exchange or calling, except if I build up myself?'"

"Have you money to begin with?"

"No, however I will have it."

"How are you going to get it?"

"I will advise you privately; I have an affluent old auntie, and she will pass on quite soon; yet in the event that she doesn't, I hope to locate some rich elderly person who will loan me two or three thousands to give me a beginning. On the off chance that I just get the cash to begin with I will progress admirably."

There is no more noteworthy error than when a youngster accepts he will prevail with acquired cash. Also, observe that this sort of discussion is as yet rehashed even into the 21st century.

Why? Since each man's experience concurs with that of Mr. Astor, who stated, "it was more hard for him to gather his initial thousand dollars, than all the succeeding millions that made up his enormous fortune." Cash is worthless except if you know the estimation of it by experience. Give a kid 20,000 dollars and put him in business, and the odds are that he will lose each dollar of it before he is a year more established. Like purchasing a ticket in the lottery; and drawing a prize, it is "what was easy to get is just as easy to lose." He doesn't have the foggiest idea about its estimation; nothing merits anything, except if it costs exertion. Without abstemiousness and economy; persistence and tirelessness, and initiating with capital which you have not procured, you don't know to prevail with regards to gathering. Youngsters, rather than "sitting tight for dead men's shoes," should be up and doing, for there is no class of people who are so unaccommodating as to passing on as these rich elderly folks individuals, and it is blessed for the hopeful beneficiaries that it is so.

The vast majority of the rich men of our nation today, begun in life as helpless young men, with decided wills, industry, determination, economy and great propensities. They went on progressively, brought in their own cash and saved it; and this is the most ideal approach to secure a fortune. Stephen Girard began life as a helpless lodge kid, and kicked the bucket worth 9,000,000 dollars. A.T. Stewart was a helpless Irish kid; and he paid assessments on a million and a half dollars of pay, every year. John Jacob Astor was a helpless rancher kid, and kicked the bucket worth twenty millions. Cornelius Vanderbilt started life paddling a boat from Staten Island to New York; he gave our administration a steamship worth 1,000,000 of dollars, and passed on worth fifty million. "There is no regal street to learning," says the maxim, and I may state it is similarly evident, "there is no illustrious street to riches." However I think there is an imperial street to both. The street to learning is an illustrious one; the street that empowers the understudy to extend his acumen and add each day to his supply of information, until, in the charming cycle of scholarly development, he can take care of the most significant issues, to check the stars, to investigate each iota of the globe, and to quantify the atmosphere this is a lofty expressway, and it is the solitary street worth voyaging.

So concerning abundance: go on in certainty, study the standards, or more all things, study human instinct; for "the legitimate investigation of humankind is man," and you will find that while growing the mind and the muscles, your expanded experience will empower you consistently to amass increasingly more head, which will build itself by premium and something else, until you show up at a condition of autonomy. You will discover, as something overall, that the helpless young men get rich and the rich young men get poor.

For example, a rich man at his perish, leaves a huge domain to his family. His oldest children, who have assisted him with procuring his fortune, know by experience the estimation of cash; and they take their legacy and add to it. The different segments of the small kids are set at revenue, and the little colleagues are applauded, and told twelve times each day, "you are rich; you will never need to work, you can generally have whatever you wish, for you were brought into the world with a brilliant spoon in your mouth." The youthful beneficiary before long discovers what that implies; he has the best dresses and toys; he is packed with sugar confections and nearly "made friends, not enemies," and he passes from school to class, petted and complimented. He gets egotistical and self-vain, manhandles his educators, and conveys everything with a high hand. He remains unaware of the genuine estimation of cash, having never acquired any; however he thoroughly understands the "brilliant spoon" business. At school, he welcomes his helpless individual understudies to his room, where he "wines and feasts" them. He is wheedled and touched, and called a magnificent decent follow, on the grounds that he is so sumptuous of his cash. He gives his game dinners, drives his quick ponies, welcomes his mates to fetes and gatherings, resolved to have bunches of "good occasions." He goes through the night in skips around and lewdness, and opens his allies with the natural tune, "we won't return home till morning." He gets them to go along with him in pulling down signs, taking entryways from their pivots and tossing them into patios and pony lakes. In the event that the police capture them, he wrecks them, is taken to the lockup, and euphorically foots the bills.

He may all the more genuinely state, "in the event that you can't make a dolt of yourself;" however he is "quick," abhors moderate things, and doesn't "see it." Youngsters stacked down with others' cash are practically certain to lose all they acquire, and they get a wide range of unfortunate propensities which, in most of cases, ruin them in wellbeing, satchel and character. In this nation, one age follows another, and the poor of today are wealthy in the future, or the third. Their experience drives them on, and they become rich, and they leave tremendous wealth to their small kids. These youngsters, having been raised in extravagance, are unpracticed and get poor; and after long experience another age goes ahead and gets together wealth again thusly.

In this conservative nation, the man makes the business. Regardless of whether he is a smithy, a shoemaker, a rancher, investor or legal advisor, inasmuch as his business is real, he might be a respectable man. So any "authentic" business is a twofold gift it helps the man occupied with it, and furthermore helps other people. The Rancher bolsters his own family, yet he additionally benefits the dealer or repairman who needs the results of his homestead. The tailor earns enough to pay the rent by his exchange, however he additionally benefits the rancher, the priest and other people who can't make their own apparel. Yet, every one of these classes regularly might be refined men.

complimented. He gets haughty and self-prideful, mishandles his educators, and conveys everything with a high hand. He remains unaware of the genuine estimation of cash, having never procured any; however he thoroughly understands the "brilliant spoon" business. At school, he welcomes his helpless individual understudies to his room, where he "wines and feasts" them. He is coaxed and touched, and called a magnificent decent follow, in light of the fact that he is so rich of his cash. He gives his game dinners, drives his quick ponies, welcomes his mates to fetes and gatherings, resolved to have bunches of "good occasions." He goes through the night in skips around and lewdness, and begins his allies with the recognizable tune, "we won't return home till morning." He gets them to go along with him in pulling down signs, taking entryways from their pivots and tossing them into lawns and pony lakes. On the off chance that the police capture them, he wrecks them, is taken to the lockup, and happily foots the bills.

He may all the more genuinely state, "in the event that you can't make a nitwit of yourself;" yet he is "quick," loathes moderate things, and doesn't "see it." Youngsters stacked down with others' cash are practically certain to lose all they acquire, and they gain a wide range of unfortunate propensities which, in most of cases, ruin them in wellbeing, tote and character. In this nation, one age follows another, and the poor of today are wealthy in the future, or the third. Their experience drives them on, and they become rich, and they leave tremendous wealth to their little youngsters. These youngsters, having been raised in extravagance, are unpracticed and get poor; and after long experience another age goes ahead and gets together wealth again thus. Also, subsequently "history rehashes itself," and cheerful is he who by tuning in to the experience of others maintains a strategic distance from the stones and sandbars on which so many have been destroyed. In this conservative nation, the man makes the business. Regardless of whether he is a metal forger, a shoemaker, a rancher, financier or legal advisor, inasmuch as his business is real, he might be a noble man. So any "authentic" business is a twofold gift it helps the man occupied with it, and furthermore helps other people. The Rancher underpins his own family, yet he additionally benefits the vendor or repairman who needs the results of his homestead. The tailor gets by his exchange, yet he likewise benefits the rancher, the priest and other people who can't make their own attire. Yet, every one of these classes regularly might be courteous fellows.

No calling, exchange, or calling, is packed in the upper story. Any place you locate the most legit and shrewd trader or investor, or the best attorney, the best specialist, the best priest, the best shoemaker, woodworker, or whatever else, that man is generally looked for, and has in every case enough to do. As a country, Americans are excessively shallow—they are endeavoring to get rich rapidly, and don't for the most part do their business as generously and completely as they should, yet whoever dominates all others in his own line, if his propensities are acceptable and his respectability undoubted, can't neglect to make sure about bountiful support, and the abundance that normally follows. Let your witticism at that point consistently be "Excelsior," for by satisfying it there is no such word as fall flat

LEARN SOMETHING USEFUL

Each man should cause his child or girl to become familiar with some helpful exchange or calling, so that in these long periods of changing fortunes of being rich to-day and helpless tomorrow they may have something substantial to fall back upon. This arrangement may save numerous people from hopelessness, who by some surprising turn of fortune have lost every one of their methods.

LET HOPE PREDOMINATE, BUT BE NOT TOO VISIONARY

Numerous people are constantly kept poor, since they are excessively visionary. Each undertaking looks to them like certain achievement, and in this manner they continue changing starting with one business then onto the next, consistently in steaming hot water, consistently "under the harrow." The arrangement of "checking the chickens before they are incubated" is a mistake of old date, however it doesn't appear to improve by age.

DO NOT DISPERSE YOUR POWERS AND IDEAS

Participate in one sort of business in particular, and stick to it reliably until you succeed, or until your experience shows that you should desert it. A consistent pounding on one nail will by and large drive it home finally, so it tends to be secured. At the point when a man's full focus is fixated on one article, his psyche will continually be proposing enhancements of significant worth, which would get away from him if his mind was involved by twelve unique subjects without a moment's delay. Numerous a fortune has gotten past a man became he was occupied with an excessive number of occupations all at once. There is acceptable sense in the old alert against having too much going on all at once immediately.

BE SYSTEMATIC

Men should be deliberate in their business. An individual who works together by rule, having a period and spot for everything, accomplishing his work expeditiously, will achieve twice so much and with a large portion of the difficulty of him who does it indiscreetly and slipshod. By bringing framework into every one of your exchanges, doing each thing in turn, continually meeting meetings with reliability, you discover relaxation for hobby and entertainment; while the one who just half does a certain something, and afterward goes to something different, and half does that, will have his business at last details, and will never know when his day's worth of effort is done, for it never will be finished. Obviously, there is a cutoff to every one of these standards. We should attempt to save the fair compromise, for there is such an incredible concept as being excessively deliberate. There are people, for example, who set aside things so cautiously that they can never discover them again. It is an excessive amount of like the "administrative noise" custom at Washington, and Mr. Dickens' "Diversion Office,"— all hypothesis and no outcome.

READ THE DAILY PAPERS

Continuously take a reliable paper, and subsequently update altogether as often as possible concerning the exchanges of the world. He who is without a paper is cut off from his species. In these days of the Web, numerous significant innovations and upgrades in each part of exchange are being made, and he who don't counsel the papers will before long get himself and his business abandoned. That is all.

BEWARE OF "OUTSIDE OPERATIONS OR UNDERTAKINGS"

We now and then observe men who have acquired fortunes, out of nowhere become poor. By and large, this emerges from lack of restraint, and regularly from gaming, and other negative behavior patterns. Habitually it happens on the grounds that a man has been occupied with "outside tasks," or the like. At the point when he gets wealthy in his real business, he is recounted a fabulous theory where he can make a score of thousands. He is continually complimented by his companions, who reveal to him that he is brought into the world fortunate, that all that he contacts transforms into gold. Presently in the event that he fails to remember that his prudent propensities, his integrity of lead and an individual consideration regarding a business which he comprehended, caused his achievement throughout everyday life, he will tune in to the alarm voices.

A couple of days slip by and it is found he should place in 10,000 dollars more: not long after he is advised "it is okay," yet certain issues not predicted, require a development of 20,000 dollars more, which will present to him a rich gather; yet before the opportunity arrives around to understand, the air pocket blasts, he loses all he is equipped with, and afterward he realizes what he should have known at the principal, that anyway effective a man might be in his own business, on the off chance that he abandons that and connects sick a business which he don't comprehend, he resembles Samson when shorn of his bolts his solidarity has left, and he becomes like different men.

On the off chance that a man has a lot of cash, he should put something in all that seems to guarantee achievement, and that will presumably profit humanity; however let the aggregates hence put be moderate in sum, and never let a man absurdly risk a fortune that he has procured m a genuine way, by contributing it m things m which he has had no insight.

DON'T INDORSE WITHOUT SECURITY OR HAVING COMPLETE CONFIDENTIALITY OR PROTECTION

No man should actually to indorse a note or become security, for any man, be it his dad or sibling, to a more prominent degree than he can bear to lose and think nothing about, without taking great security. Here is a man that is worth 20,000 dollars; he is doing a flourishing assembling or commercial exchange; you are resigned and living on your cash; he comes to you and says:

"You know that I am worth 20,000 dollars, and don't owe a dollar; on the off chance that I had 5,000 dollars in real money, I could buy a specific part of merchandise and twofold my cash in two or three months; will you indorse my note for that sum?"

You mirror that he is worth 20,000 dollars, and you cause no danger by supporting his note; you like to oblige him, and you loan your name without avoiding potential risk of getting security. Not long after, he shows you the note with your support dropped, and advises you, most likely genuinely, "that he made the benefit that he expected by the activity," you mirror that you have done a decent activity, and the idea causes you to feel cheerful. Eventually, something very similar happens again and you do it once more; you have just fixed the impression in your psyche that it is completely protected to indorse his notes without security.

However, the difficulty is, this man is getting cash too without any problem. He has just to count on your note, get it limited and take the money. He gets cash for now without exertion; without burden to himself. Presently mark the outcome. He sees an opportunity for theory outside of his business. A brief speculation of just $10,000 is required. It makes certain to return before a note at the bank would be expected. He puts a note for that sum before you. You sign it precisely. Being immovably persuaded that your companion is dependable and reliable; you indorse his notes as a "the usual result."

Shockingly the hypothesis doesn't reach a critical stage so soon as was normal, and another $10,000 note should be limited to take up the last one when due. Before this note develops the hypothesis has demonstrated an absolute disappointment and all the cash is lost. Does the washout tell his companion, the endorser, that he has lost portion of his fortune? Not under any condition. He don't make reference to that he has estimated by any means. However, he has energized; the soul of hypothesis has held onto him; he sees others making enormous totals along these lines (we rarely know about the failures), and, as different examiners, he "searches for his cash where he loses it." He attempts once more. underwriting notes has gotten constant with you, and at each misfortune he gets your mark for however much he needs. At long last you find your companion has lost the entirety of his property and the entirety of yours. You are overpowered with wonder and anguish, and you state "it is something hard; my companion here has destroyed me," however, you should add, "I have additionally demolished him." In the event that you had said in any case, "I will oblige you, yet I never indorse without taking abundant security," he was unable to have gone past the length of his tie, and he couldn't have ever been enticed away from his real business. It is something risky, along these lines, whenever, to allow individuals to get ownership of cash too effectively; it entices them to unsafe theories, if that's it.

So with the youngster beginning in business; let him comprehend the estimation of cash by acquiring it. At the point when he comprehends its worth, at that point oil the wheels a little in assisting him with beginning business, however recall, men who get cash with too incredible office can't generally succeed. You should get the main dollars by harsh times, and at some penance, to like the estimation of those dollars.

ADVERTISE YOUR BUSINESS VERY EFFICIENTLY AND WISELY

We as a whole depend, pretty much, upon the general population for our help. We as a whole exchange with general society—legal counselors, specialists, shoemakers, craftsmen, metal forgers, actors, show stagers, railroad presidents, and school teachers. The individuals who manage the public should be cautious that their merchandise are important; that they are certifiable, and will give fulfillment. At the point when you get an article which you know is going to satisfy your clients, and that when they have attempted it, they will feel they have their cash's worth, at that point let the reality be realized that you have it. Be mindful so as to promote it in some shape or other in light of the fact that it is obvious that if a man has great an article available to be purchased, and no one knows it, it will present to him no return.

Where almost everyone peruses, and where papers are given and coursed in versions of 5,000 to 200,000, it would be hasty if this channel was not exploited to arrive at general society in promoting. A paper goes into the family, and is perused by spouse and kids, just as the top of the home; thus hundreds and thousands of individuals may peruse your promotion, while you are taking care of your normal business. Some, maybe, read it while you are sleeping. The entire way of thinking of life is, first "sow," at that point "procure." That is the manner in which the rancher does; he plants his potatoes and corn, and sows his grain, and afterward approaches something different, and the opportunity arrives when he harvests. Yet, he never harvests first and sows a while later. This guideline applies to a wide range of business, and to nothing more prominently than to publicizing. In the event that a man has a real article, its absolutely impossible wherein he can harvest more profitably than by "planting" to the general population thusly. He should, obviously, have a great article, and one which will satisfy his clients; anything misleading won't succeed for all time in light of the fact that the general population is more astute than many envision. People are childish, and we as a whole favor buying where we can take full advantage of our cash and we attempt to discover where we can most without a doubt do as such.

You may promote a fake article, and actuate numerous individuals to call and get it once, however they will revile you as an impostor and backstabber, and your

business will slowly vanish and leave you poor. This is correct. Barely any individuals can securely rely on possibility custom. All of you need to have your clients return and buy once more.

So a man who publicizes at all should keep it up until the public know who and what he is, and what his business is, or, more than likely the cash put resources into promoting is lost.

A few men have a curious virtuoso for composing a striking ad, one that will capture the consideration of the peruser from the outset sight. This reality, obviously, gives the publicist an extraordinary bit of leeway. In some cases a man makes himself mainstream by a novel sign or an inquisitive presentation in his window.

BE POLITE AND KIND TO YOUR CUSTOMERS

Good manners and politeness are the best capital ever put resources into business. Huge stores, plated signs, flaring commercials, will all demonstrate unavailing on the off chance that you or your representatives treat your supporters unexpectedly. Truly, the more kind and liberal a man is the more liberal will be the support presented to him. Like sires like. The one who gives the best measure of merchandise of a relating quality for the least whole (actually saving for himself a benefit) will for the most part succeed best over the long haul. This carries us to the brilliant standard, "As ye would that men ought to never really, do ye likewise to them" and they will improve by you than if you generally regarded them as though you needed to get the most you could out of them for the least return.

Men who drive sharp deals with their clients, going about as though they never expected to see them again, won't be mixed up. They will never observe them again as clients.

BE CHARITABLE AND VERY GIVING

Obviously men should be beneficent, in light of the fact that it is an obligation and a delight. Yet, even as an issue of strategy, in the event that you have no higher impetus, you will find that the liberal man will order support, while the shameful, uncharitable grumpy person will be dodged.

Solomon says: "There is that scattereth but increaseth; and there is that withholdeth more than meet, yet it tendeth to destitution." obviously the solitary genuine cause is what is from the heart.

The most ideal sort of noble cause is to help the individuals who are eager to help themselves. Unbridled almsgiving, without inquisitive into the value of the candidate, is awful in each sense. Yet, to look out and unobtrusively help the individuals who are battling for themselves, is the sort that dissipate but increment. In any case, don't fall into the possibility that a few people practice, of giving a supplication rather than a potato, and an invocation rather than bread, to the hungry. It is simpler to make Christians with full stomachs than void.

DON'T BLAB UNNECESSARILY

A few men have a silly propensity for confessing their business insider facts. On the off chance that they bring in cash they like to tell their neighbors how it was finished. Nothing is picked up by this, and frequently much is lost. Say nothing regarding your benefits, your expectations, your assumptions, your goals. Also, this ought to apply to letters just as to discussion.

Financial specialists should compose letters, however they should be cautious what they put in them. In the event that you are losing cash, be particularly careful and not recount it, or you will lose your standing.

PRESERVE YOUR INTEGRITY

Honesty is more valuable than jewels or rubies. This exhortation was abominably mischievous, however it was the very quintessence of ineptitude: It was as much as to state in the event that you think that its hard to get cash truly, you can undoubtedly get it deceptively. Not to realize that the most troublesome thing in life is to bring in cash insincerely!

Not to realize that our jails are loaded with men who endeavored to follow this exhortation; not to comprehend that no man can be deceptive, without before long being discovered, and that when his absence of standard is found, essentially every road to progress is shut against him until the end of time. The public appropriately avoid all whose uprightness is questioned. Regardless of how neighborly and wonderful and obliging a man might be, none of us try to manage him in the event that we suspect "bogus loads and measures." Severe trustworthiness, not just lies at the establishment of all accomplishment throughout everyday life (monetarily), however in each other regard.

Firm respectability of character is significant. It makes sure about to its owner a harmony and delight which can't be accomplished without it— which no measure of cash, or houses and terrains can buy. A man who is known to be carefully genuine, might be poor, yet he has the totes of all the network available to him—for all realize that in the event that he vows to restore what he gets, he will never disillusion them. As a simple matter of self-centeredness, in this way, if a man had no higher intention in being straightforward, all will find that the saying of Dr. Franklin can never neglect to be valid, that "trustworthiness is the best strategy."

To get rich, isn't generally equal to being fruitful. "There are numerous rich helpless men," while there are numerous others, genuine and ardent people, who have never had such a lot of cash as some rich people waste in seven days, however who are in any case truly more extravagant and more joyful than any man can actually be while he is a violator of the higher laws of his being.

The excessive love of cash, almost certainly, might be and is "the foundation of all insidious," however cash itself, when appropriately utilized, isn't just a "convenient thing to have in the house," yet manages the cost of the delight of gift our race by empowering its owner to broaden the extent of human joy and human impact. The longing for abundance is almost general, and none can say it isn't praiseworthy, given its owner acknowledges its duties, and utilizations it as a companion to humankind.

The historical backdrop of obtaining riches, which is business, is a past filled with human advancement, and any place exchange has prospered most, there, as well, have workmanship and science created the noblest natural products. Truth be told, as something overall, cash getters are the advocates of our race. To them, in an incredible measure, are we obligated for our establishments of learning and of craftsmanship, our foundations, schools and houses of worship. It is no contention against the craving for, or the ownership of riches, to state that there are in some cases grumpy persons who crowd cash just for storing and who have no higher goal than to get a handle on all that which goes inside their scope. As we have once in a while two-timers in religion, and revolutionaries in governmental issues, so there are incidentally penny pinchers among, cash getters. These, in any case, are just special cases for the overall principle. In any case, when, in this nation, we find such a disturbance and hindrance as a misanthrope, we recall with appreciation that in America we have no laws of primogeniture, and that in the proper way of nature the opportunity will come when the accumulated residue will be dissipated to serve humankind.

To all people: bring in cash truly, and not something else, for Shakespeare has genuinely stated, "He that needs cash, means, and substance, is without three old buddies."